CUMBRIAN ENGLISH

Compiled by William & Betsy Bell

ABSON BOOKS LONDON

5 Sidney Square London E1 2EY
Tel 020 7790 4737
Fax 020 7790 7346
email absonbooks@aol.com
web www.absonbooks.co.uk

ABSON BOOKS LONDON
First published June 2008
© W & B Bell
Design by Creative Mouse Ltd
Cover photo by John Lilley

Printed by
Guttenberg Press, Malta
ISBN 978 0902920 804

INTRODUCTION

Important though it is for Cumbrians near and far to remember their roots with the sight and sound of dialect words and phrases, it also gives them provenance of who they are and where they have come from. It is hoped that the many visitors to Cumbria will want to retain a memory of this dialect also, which is the purpose of this little glossary.

Cumbrians have inherited an interesting and diverse dialect that is unique. Its purest form is clearly that of the central core of the hills and valleys but has, at the perimeters, been greatly influenced by the counties of Lancashire, Yorkshire, Durham, Northumberland and Scotland.

Before the arrival of the roman emperor Hadrian, the people of Cumberland belonged to a Celtic Carvetii tribe who later joined up with a bigger Iron Age tribe called Brigantes. They spoke a form of Brythonic Celtic that was known as Cumbric.

The arrival, via Ireland, of the Norsemen in the 8th century made a big impact on the words and language of Cumberland. When they left in the 12th century there remained many words, some of which are still used today like *lonnin* (lane) and *thwaite* (meadow).

From the c1600 Cumberland was home to many immigrants from Cornwall, Wales, Ireland and Germany seeking employment in the iron ore, coal, copper and wadd mines. This had a small impact on the dialect overall but more so in North and West Cumberland.

The present County of Cumbria was only created in 1974 by the amalgamation of Westmorland with Cumberland and the addition of parts of North Lancashire but the dialect lives on and we hope that everyone will enjoy our selection of these words and phrases.

A

abackerbeyont	behind, remote area, as *t' back o'Skidda*
abeun	above
aboot	about
addle	earn a living
afoar	before, as *git thee clogs on afoar thoos gaars oot*
allus	always
anunder	beneath
Ah'm garn yam	I'm off home
auld	old
awez	come on

B

back'ander	slap, as *thoo'll git a back 'ander if thoo does'nt button lip*
backword	change of mind
badly	not feeling too well
bairn	child
bait	workman's packed lunch kept in a bait box
bandy-legged	bowed legged person
Bassenthat Lyke	Bassenthwaite Lake
beck	stream, as in Caldbeck, Millbeck
bez'lin	drinking, as *thoos allus bez'lin*
biddies	fleas or old women
blea	blue as *bleaberries*
blether	nonsense talk, as *will t'stop thee bletherin'*

boddy	senior citizen, as *grand auld boddy*
boggle	spirit of mystical animals historically seen at Hodgin How
Booder Stean	Bowder Stone
bowk	to puke
brant	steep
braffin	horse collar used to frame bizarre faces, called gurning
brat	apron
bray	hit with fists
Braythet	Braithwaite
breet	bright
brocken	broken, as *yon yat's brocken*
brossen	eaten too much, as *Ah'm fare brossen noo efter t' Tatie Pot*
browt	brought
brudder	brother

bubble	cry, as *stop thee bubbling*
byre	indoor building for cows
byuk	book

C

Cat Bells	mountain overlooking Derwentwater, was the den of the wildcats
cample	argue
canny	careful, as *she's a canny lass*
Casle'ead	Castlehead, near Keswick, thought to be an ancient volcanic plug
caulkers	iron rims for wooden clogs
chang	uproar, incoherent chatter

chess	chase
chucken	leaving, as *it's aboot chucken oot time*
chuddy	chewing gum
clarty	sticky, as *yon gingerbread is reet clarty*
clemmed	thirsty, as *Ah'm fare clemmed*
cloot	slap or hit someone, as *he gev him a reet cloot*
clout	cloth, as *nare cast a clout till t'May be oot*
codge-up	poor workmanship by rogue builders
coo-clap	cow dung
crack	chat, as *ah've hed a bit of a crack wi her*
crag rat	enthusiastic rock climber
cross buttock	Cumbrian wrestling term
Crosthet	Crosthwaite
cuddy	donkey, as *hes ta' ivver seen a cuddy lowp a five barr'd yat?*
cwoat	coat

D

daft ha'porth	friendly riposte to an unwise person
dander	temper, as *he's reet got 'is dander up*
dang	damn it
deed	dead
deek	sly look around
Derwentwatter	Derwentwater
diun	done
divvent	don't, as *divvent bother theesenn*
dodder	tremble
dook	swim, as *ista gaan dooking in t' lake?*
dookers	swimming trunks

dub	pool in a stream
dusta ken?	do you know?
dyke	hedge, as *wuz thoo wi oor Elsie t' back yon dyke yisterdah?*

E

eddle	earn
eee ah sae	surprised to learn something
e'e-breeas	eyebrows
efter	after, as *what's thoo efter noo?*
enuff	enough, *as ista hed enuff?*
etlins	income from work done

F

fadder	father
fair bit o'crack	a good old gossip
fare	completely, *as ah'm fare worn oot*
fash	worry, bother, *as divvent fash theesenn*
feat	foot
firtle	mess about
flate	frightened
flea pie	currant cake
fisslen	buzzing, *as yon flea's fisslen aboot in t'back kitchen*
flaach	persuade
flaysome	hideous
flummoxed	bothered, *as ah'm reet flummoxed*
foisty	musty

forbrest	directly in front
fothering	feeding animals by hand
frae	from, *as ah'm frae Braythet, where's thoo frae?*
fratch	argue
full up	brought to tears, *as ah'm reet full oop, t'wife's left ma*
fwolk	folk

G

galluses	braces for holding your *keks* up
gammy	injured limb, *as oor Rachel hes a reet gammy leg*
gander	to have a look at something
ganzee	jumper or jacket for extra warmth
gaan	going, *as how's t'gaan?*

gar	go
garrak	awkward or clumsy person
gauk	cack-handed, a left handed person
gawkin	looking around in a confused way
ginnel	alleyway, between buildings
girt	big, as *yon Jimmy's a girt lad*
git	get
goosegobs	gooseberries
gowk	cuckoo
gripe	complain, as *what's t'gripin' on aboot?*
gurning	making a hideous face

H

happen	possibly, maybe, as *happen ye'll len ma a tenner?*
harpin' on	insisting upon something
Herdwick sheep	An ancient breed of Cumbrian sheep of Celtic/Norse origin. (See page 34)
hesta	have you, as *hesta t' time a day?*
heed	head
helm wind	cold easterly wind
hitty-missy	unreliable, as *it's a bit hitty missy*
hod on	just a minute, as *willsta hod on lad*
hogg	young Herdwick of six to fifteen months
hod thee whisht	stop jabberin on
hoo	how
hoo's t' gaan on marra?	*how are you mate?,* especially from West Cumbria

hoo's thi fettal?	*how are you doing?*
hoond Trail	hound dog race involving much betting and monetary prizes for the winners

I

ilk	family, as *she's yan o' t' siam ilk*
I'll gar wi' thee	I will go with you
inklin	hint, idea, as *ah've hed an inklin aboot it*
ista	are you, as *ista gaan t' Ke-zick?*
ist'er?	is there, as *ist'er owt left in t' pot?*
ivver	ever
ivv'rybody	everybody, as *ivv'rybody hes t' hev sumbody*

J

jabber	talk, as *he's niver done jabberin'*
jerkin	jacket
jerry	pub, as *ah'm gaan t'Portinskeal jerry*
jeyk	squeak, like a new pair of shoes
jiggen	fussing around, as *thoo's jiggen aboot a lot t'day*
jiggered	tired
jip	pain, as *t' lad's back's givin' im sum jip*
joggle	loose
joggly	unlevel, as *ah'm gaan doon yon joggly rood taneet*

K

kaisty	pernickety about eating
kak-handed	left-handed
kaylied	drunk, as *let's gar yam, thoo's reet kaylied*
Keks	trousers
ken	know, as *dusta ken John Peel?*
kern supper	corn, celebration of the harvest
Kessick Codlin	18th century apple
ketkite	a mean person
Ke-zick	Keswick
kilter	out of order, as *ah'm reet oot t' kilter after yisterdah*
knocken-on	getting older, as *oor fadder's knocken' on a bit*
kyaks	cakes

L

laal	small or little
laik	play about, as *he's off t'park ta laik aboot*
lang	long
lehk	look
leet	light
lish	nimble, supple
liggen	lying, as *she's liggen int' bed just noo*
living over t' brush	unmarried partners
lonnin	lane
lowp	jump
lowsed	turned loose, *Herdwick tups a' lowsed in t' back end aboot November*
lugs	ears
lumpheed	silly person

M

ma	me
madder	mother
maffled	perplexed, bewildered
marra	mate
mash	making a pot o tea
masher	a smart lad
mekkin	making
mend	improved health, as *Ars on t'mend noo*
middin	historical farmyard area for animal waste and composting
middlin	about average, as *he's just fair t'middlin at present*
mizzlin	fine drops of rain, as *it's mizzlin a bit ootside*
miunleet flit	moonlight flit, overnight disappearance

mot	woman or girlfriend
muck-sweat	maximum perspiration, as *ah'm in a reet muck-sweat t'present*
mun	mouth, as *willsta shut thi mun*
munnet	must not

N

nare	never
naws	knows
nay	no, as *nay matter*
neb	nose
neet	night, as *it's a grand neet t'neet*

nesh	feeling delicate
nigh on	almost, as *it's nigh on midneet*
nip	tiny measure, quantity
nivver	never
nobbut	only, as *dusta ken it's nobbut ten o'clock?*
noo	now, as *noo then what's t' gaan on aboot?*
nowt	nothing

O

oor	our/family member, as *oor Eddie's gaan fishin'*
oot o' fettle	feeling unwell, as *oor Pam's reet oot o'fettle*
ow do	hello there
ower theer	over there

owt	anything
owz it gaan?	how's it going?
oxter	armpit

P

paggered	very tired, as *ah'm reet paggered*
parlish	amazing
pecker	courage, as *keep thee pecker up lad*
Peerith	Penrith
perishen	hungry, as *ah'm fare perishen*
pickle	predicament, as *oor Jo's in't reet pickle*
plugger	idiot

pleen	complain
posser	wooden tool used for laundry
puir	poor
pund	pound sterling

Q

| quaveren | sparring |
| quiff | wave, as *thoo's a reet masher wi t'quiff in' t'hair* |

R

radge	senseless, idiotic
ratch	look, as *he's ratching aboot a bit*
rang	wrong
reet	right, as *it wuz a reet good doo last neet*
reetle	smooth, as *will'ta reetle t'bed a bit?*
riddance	get rid of, as *gud riddance t' bad rubbish*
rood	road
rot-gut	bad ale
rig-ma-rowl	verbal excesses
Rosthet	Rosthwaite, Borrowdale
rum butter	Cumbrian delicacy for Christmas & christenings
rum do	odd or curious affair

S

sarrad	satisfied, as *efter t' meal he wez reet weel sarrad*
Scafell Pike	*Scawfell Pike,* highest mountain in England
Sca Fell	*Scaw Fell,* neighbour of the Pike
scheal	school
scop	throw
scowpin	picking something up
scram	rind on bacon, clear off
scrattin	looking for, as *he's scrattin roond a bit*
scrow	mess, as *thoos left a reet scrow in t'kitchen*
scrunt	apple core
scrumping	stealing, as *tekkin apples*
Seathet	Seathwaite, Borrowdale,
sen	since, as *she passed away ten years sen*

setten-on	got a job
shillies	small stones by the edge of a lake
siam	same
skemmy	beer
skit	make fun of
sleck	slake, as *ah'll sleck me thirst wi sum yal*
skelp	slap
slopst'ne	old kitchen sink
smocked-faced	clean shaven, as *yon fella's varra smocked faced*
snaps	hard baked gingerbread
snag	pull up root vegetables
sneck	door latch
Speeatry	Aspatria
Steanth'te	Stonethwaite in Borrowdale
strinkle	sprinkle
summat	something, as *git summat for t' bait*

T

t'	the, as *t'summer is a cummin*
taneet	tonight, as *ista gaan oot taneet?*
Tatie-pot	traditional Cumbrian dish of meat & vegitables
t'backend	autumn time
teeming	heavy rain, as *it's reet teeming doon*
tek hod	take hold, wrestling term
tekken	very attentive, as *he's fair tekken wi oor Jean*
tekkin	taking
tha	you
thee	you, as *ah'm not sure aboot thee*
thi	your, as *put thi best ganzee on*
think on	don't forget, as *think on noo*
thirit	thirtieth

thissenn	yourself
thoo	you, as *thoo naws nowt aboot owt*
thowt	thought
thrang	busy
thwaite	meadow, as in *Stonethwaite, Seathwaite, etc*
traipse	wandering about
tup	ram
tupping time	procreational activities for sheep around November
twat	to hit, as *he's givin im a reet twat*
twentit	twentieth
twine	groan, as *will t'stop twinin' on*

U

unbethowt	recollected
upshaw	over, as *it's upshaw wi him*
upshot	final
unsneck	unlatch, open the door

V

varra	very

W

waat's wrang?	what's wrong, as *ist'er summat wrang?*
wad	would
waffler	change around, as *yon lad's a reet waffler*
wark	work
watter	water, as *Derwentwatter*
wedder	weather
weel	well
wesh	wash, as *ah's gaan t' hev a wesh*
whack	share, as *ah've diun me whack for noo*
whingeing	complaining
whish't	be quiet, as *hod thee whish't*
wick	remarkably fit for his or her age
willsta	will you

wimmen	women
Wukkit'n	Workington
wuz	was

Y

yal	ale
yananudder	one another
yan	one, as *let's hev yan for t' rood?*
yam	home
yance	once
yatterin	talking a lot
yat	gate

ye ken?	do you know?
ye'll	you will, as *ye'll nut forgit noo*
yisterdah	yesterday
yon	that, as *hesta seen yon coo?*
yowe	ewe, female Herdwick
yowlen	crying, as *willsta give ower yowlen*
yung	young
yuks	ties, used around trouser legs

THE NUMBERING OF HERDWICK SHEEP

The following system for counting sheep was thought to be in regular use in Borrowdale until the early nineteenth century.

1	yan	11	yan-a-dick
2	tyan	12	tyan-a-dick
3	tethera	13	tethera-a-adick
4	methera	14	methera-a-dick
5	pimp	15	bumfit
6	sethera	16	yan-a-bumfit
7	lethera	17	tyan-a-bumfit
8	hovera	18	tethera-a-bumfit
9	dovera	19	methera-a-bumfit
10	dick	20	giggot

After number twenty the system was begun again, adding each additional twenty on a finger or transferring small stones from one pocket to another

Seathwaite at Borrowdale's south end had a variation of words for the numbering.

1	aina		6	ithy
2	peina		7	mithy
3	para		8	owera
4	peddera		9	lowera
5	pimp		10	digthen

After number ten '–a-dig' was added, as aina-a-dig (11), peina-a-dig (12) etc.

OTHER TITLES AVAILABLE

Language Glossaries
American English/English American
Australian English/English Australian
Cumbrian English
Gay slang
Geordie English
Hip Hop English
Home Counties English
Irish English/English Irish
Lancashire English
Military Slang
Playground Slang & Teenspeak
Prison Slang
Rhyming Cockney Slang
Rude Rhyming Slang
Scottish English/English Scottish
Scouse English

West Country English
Yiddish English/English Yiddish
Yorkshire English

History
The Death of Kings – A history
of how the Kings & Queens of
England died

Literary Quiz & Puzzle Books
Jane Austen   Gilbert & Sullivan
Bronte Sisters   Thomas Hardy
Shakespeare

All of these titles area available from good booksellers
or by contacting the publisher:
Abson Books London 5 Sidney Square London E1 2EY
Tel 020 7790 4737 Fax 020 7790 7346
email absonbooks@aol.com
web www.absonbooks.co.uk